the**people**

the**art**

the**talk**

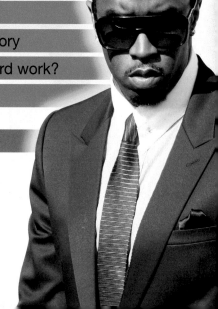

Best-dressed

It can take years to build a good reputation as a celebrity stylist. Many start by styling celebrities and models for magazines, films or television shows. They learn dressmaking skills, and become experts in putting together the right clothes to create a stunning effect. Top celebrity stylists can create looks that suit both the person and event perfectly. They get their clients on the best-dressed lists time after time.

celebrity
fashion
stylist

STANDARD LOAN

The College, Merthyr Tydfil Learnir
U   rth Wales CF4

Isabel Thomas

First published in 2015 by Wayland

Copyright © Wayland 2015

All rights reserved
Dewey Number: 746.9'2'092-dc23
ISBN: 978 0 7502 9455 3
Library ebook ISBN: 978 0 7502 7400 5

10 9 8 7 6 5 4 3 2 1

Concept by Joyce Bentley

Commissioned by Debbie Foy and
Rasha Elsaeed

Produced for Wayland by Calcium
Designer: Paul Myerscough
Editor: Sarah Eason

MIX
Paper from
responsible sources
FSC® C104740

Printed in China

Wayland is an imprint of
Hachette Children's Group
Part of Hodder & Stoughton
Carmelite House
50 Victoria Embankment
London EC4Y 0DZ

An Hachette UK Company

www.hachette.co.uk
www.hachettechildrens.co.uk

Printed in China

Acknowledgements: Dreamstime: Konradbak
cvr bg; Getty Images: 18–19, WireImage 6, 27;
Istockphoto: Andipantz 21, Izabela Habur 20–21;
Lenya Jones: 2b, 14c, 14r, 14–15, 15l, 15c; Melis
Kuris: 10, 10bl, 10bc, 10br; Shutterstock: Arvzdix 2r,
9b, Sandra Cunningham 12–13, DSPA 30bl, Helga
Esteb 1, 8r, 17t, 17b, 22–23, Fashion B 30l, Raisa
Kanareva 25, Nina Malyna 9tr, Luba V Nel 31r,
Losevsky Pavel 24, Lev Radin 23r, Rido cvr fg, Joe
Seer 3br, 22bl, 29, Kiselev Andrey Valerevich 30br,
Vipflash 2t, 4–5, Mayer George Vladimirovich 9tl,
Debby Wong 9bl, 16–17; Wikipedia: 28, Manuel
Bartual 31b.

cover stories

STAR STYLE

Celebrities are rarely photographed in the same clothes twice. How do they put together so many fresh, trendy outfits? Most have a secret weapon: a stylist. It is their job to come up with the perfect look for every appearance.

Image is everything

Celebrity stylists do not just choose clothes. They help their clients to create an image that wins them media attention, fans and work. Stylists learn to know their clients inside out. They understand how clothes work on different body shapes, and choose clothes that fit well and look great.

Get the look

Most celebrity public appearances, from red-carpet events to working out at the gym, are carefully styled. Readers of magazines, newspapers and blogs expect to see different outfits every time, so stylists are constantly working to create new looks. Top stylists do not just follow fashion trends: they make them. They influence high-street fashion, too. When fashion fans see an A-list star looking great, they want to copy the look and so stores may base a whole collection around one famous person's style.

Fashion and fame

Stylists have the power to turn products into must-have items. When fashion designers invite stars and their stylists to their shows, they hope that the celebrity will buy the clothes and then be photographed wearing them, and so create a following of fashionistas. Top stylists may help designers with their collections and can even start their own fashion lines.

BRITT BARDO

Superstar stylist

Britt winning the Star Stylist award at the 2009 Hollywood Life's Style Awards. Britt says her aim is to make her clients look 'super-relaxed and effortless'.

From farming to fashion

Britt Bardo grew up in a small farming town where there were few fashion stores, but she found creative ways to be fashionable, such as using coloured paper clips as earrings! When she was 18, she moved to Detroit, USA, and trained to be a photographer at the city's College for Creative Studies. After finishing her degree, she moved to New York City in search of work.

Big break

In New York, Britt soon realised that styling photo shoots would be the best way to combine her love of fashion and her knowledge of what makes a great picture. She first worked as a sales assistant in the designer jeans shop G-Star New York. Then she spent three years assisting celebrity stylist Andrea Lieberman, whose clients included Gwen Stefani and Jennifer Lopez. Britt's big break came when JLo asked her to be her personal stylist.

THE STATS

Name: Britt Bardo
Place of birth: Lima, Ohio, USA
Lives: Los Angeles, USA, and New York City, USA
Job: Hollywood stylist and fashion consultant

Career highlights

2004 styled the Jennifer Lopez music video for *Get Right*

2006 *Forbes* magazine called her a 'superstar stylist'

2007 styled the Mariah Carey music video for *Lil L.O.V.E*

2008 styled the Hilary Duff music video for *Reach Out*

2010 signed as fashion consultant for eBay

Fashion fun

Britt soon became known for her fun attitude to fashion and she won more famous clients, including actress Kate Hudson and stars Mary-Kate and Ashley Olsen. Britt helped the Olsen twins to work out their 'scruffy chic' look, transforming them into fashion icons.

In demand

Today, Britt is stylist to A-list stars such as Cameron Diaz and Blake Lively. But while her job has glamorous perks, such as hanging out with celebrity clients, in her spare time Britt likes to scuba dive, and spend time with her family. Her career may have sky-rocketed, but her feet are very firmly on the ground!

MAKING IT

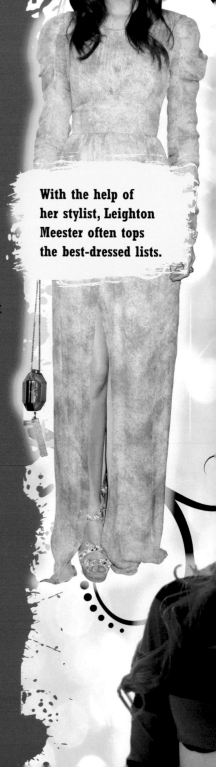

From choosing red-carpet dresses to planning a film's costumes, there are several different ways for a stylist to work with celebrities.

Dressing the stars

Celebrities use stylists to help them plan their everyday wardrobes as well as their red carpet looks. Personal stylists also help rising stars to develop a signature look. Stylists learn what suits their clients and help them to maintain a trend-setting look, making sure the paparazzi never get a bad picture.

Making up stories

Stylists such as Katie Grand, who work for magazines or newspapers, are known as fashion editors or fashion directors. Part of their job is styling models and celebrities for photoshoots. These stylists help to create a 'story' that shows both the star and the products at their best. Each shoot can take weeks of planning and a top stylist can expect to earn US$50,000 for a celebrity fashion shoot.

With the help of her stylist, Leighton Meester often tops the best-dressed lists.

Looking the part

Costume designers are stylists who create film character looks. Getting a character's look right can involve a lot of research – costume designers create anything from vampires to gangsters. The clothes worn in popular shows set fashion trends, and some actors are now as famous for their screen style as their talent – for example, *Gossip Girl* stylist Eric Daman has turned cast members Blake Lively and Leighton Meester into fashion icons.

Image makers

The stage outfits worn by pop icons such as Lady Gaga, Beyoncé and Rihanna shape their strong image. To get it right, celebrities hire creative or artistic directors to style every part of a show, from costumes to choreography. Top creative directors, such as William Baker, can be just as important to a musician's career as their record producer and publicity agents.

Fashion editors direct photoshoots to help create a theme that complements the clothes.

Beyoncé and Rihanna use artistic directors to create an on-stage style that suits their songs.

What got you interested in fashion?

Growing up in Turkey, I would change my outfit at least five times a day for every occasion. I collected vintage fashion, including amazing pieces that my parents bought in the 1960s and 1970s, from Hermès scarves to Gaultier suits.

Check out Melis' red carpet gallery at www.meliskuris.com

MELIS KURIS

Radar expert Melis Kuris has styled Anna Paquin, Cat Deeley, Ashley Greene, Lily Collins and Taylor Lautner.

How did you become a celebrity stylist?

When I was 18, I moved to Los Angeles, USA, and started working for different stylists. It was so much fun styling models for shoots and shows! I realised then that styling could be a career path for me.

What are the best parts of your job?

Every day is different, so I never get tired of working. I'm constantly collaborating with new people. One highlight of my career so far was working with most of the cast of *Twilight* for their first movie première. That job completely changed my career and I am so grateful for the experience.

Does your job have any downsides?

The downside of being a stylist is that everyone has an opinion on your work. Regardless, you have to have tough skin and stay true to yourself. You have to have confidence in what you are talking about.

What helps someone succeed in fashion styling?

Being organised. We constantly have to check in and check out clothes with fashion houses and handle receipts. If you lose something, you have to pay for it.

What's next in your career?

I like to dabble in a little bit of everything, including personal styling, magazines, advertising campaigns, commercials, music videos, TV and fashion shows. I have just finished costume designing my first film, which is exciting. I like to be the stylist who always says, 'Yes, I've done that!'

What advice do you have for someone wanting to become a stylist?

Never turn down a job. Ever. It doesn't matter if it pays a lot or absolutely nothing. If you take on a job, it may lead to something bigger.

MILLION DOLLAR LOOKS

8

The number of dresses Anne Hathaway wore to present the 2011 Academy Awards ceremony. Her outfits were chosen by stylist Rachel Zoe.

£4,000

The top daily fee charged by a celebrity stylist in the run up to the Oscars.

£7,000

The cost of hair styling, make-up, eyelash extensions and spray tanning for top celebrities on Oscar day.

3 HOURS

The average time it takes to style a female star's make-up and hair for a red-carpet ceremony.

80
PER CENT

The proportion of Hollywood stylist Nicole Chavez's clients who get to keep their gowns after a red carpet event.

£19,000

The amount earned by a top costume designer per project.

£32,000

The amount earned by a top stylist for several weeks' work planning a fashion shoot with a celebrity client.

HOLLYWOOD DREAMS

My story by Lenya Jones

I've always loved fashion, but at first I didn't know how I could make a career out of it. When I was younger, I worked as a marketing assistant at a famous department store in Sydney, Australia, that was often featured in fashion magazines. I started to get ideas about styling and one of my managers persuaded me to try my hand at it.

To get a better understanding of the job, I started assisting stylists. Assisting is the best way to learn because you get hands-on experience. When I felt I was ready, I started approaching photographers and began test shooting like crazy. Then, an Australian magazine called *Cherrie* asked me to organise their fashion section. After that, I was hired to style more fashion spreads and my work appeared in magazines regularly.

Next, a TV director asked me to work on the wardrobe for a TV pilot. I was lucky enough to work with a world-famous assistant director and an amazing producer, who recommended me for other projects, including a short film. After that, I worked on several films and TV adverts, dressing the stars and making everyone look great. My first feature film *Dealing with Destiny* (2011) even premièred at the Cannes Film Festival.

Now, I'm pursuing more costume designing opportunities in Hollywood, and plan to move to Los Angeles, USA. With perseverance and determination, I hope to hold the Oscar for Best Costume Design in the near future! My top tip is: don't give up. If you really love styling, just go for it!

Follow Lenya's blog and work at www.lenyajones.com

RED CARPET TRICKS

Radar reveals the stylists' tricks that keep celebrities looking perfectly groomed on the red carpet.

1. Wig tape

The double-sided sticky tape used to keep wigs in place is a last-minute style saver. Wig tape has amazing holding power and can be cut to any shape. Stylists use it to mend broken hemlines, stick feathers or flowers in place, and keep clothes in the right place as the celebrity waves to the crowd.

2. Needle and nylon thread

If a celebrity looks like she is sewn into her dress, she probably is! Stylists always have a needle and strong thread at hand to mend broken zips, straps, or jewellery. Clear nylon thread is invisible to the cameras, so no one will know that the star had to be cut out of their outfit at the end of the night!

3. Sandpaper

New shoes are a must for the red carpet, but slippery soles and soft carpet can add up to disaster. Stylists use sandpaper to scratch the bottom of shoes and prevent slipping.

4. Make-up sponge

Deodorant is a must for nerve-wracking award shows, which involve sitting for hours under hot lights. Celebrity stylists have a clever trick to remove deodorant marks from expensive dresses. A clean and dry make-up sponge can remove white marks gently, without needing to use water. The sponges are small enough for the star to slip into her handbag for emergency touch-ups.

5. Tumble dryer sheet

On a hot, dry day, flyaway hair can ruin a celebrity's red carpet look. Some stylists use a bizarre trick. They touch the hair very lightly with a tumble dryer sheet. This gets rid of the static electricity that creates frizz, just like it does with the laundry!

WILLIAM BAKER

THE STATS

Name: William Baker
Born: 1973
Place of birth: Manchester, UK
Nationality: British
Job: Personal stylist and creative director

Stylish start

William grew up in Manchester, UK. In the 1980s, the stylish city was home to world-famous nightclubs and bands. William became well-known on the style scene, but also worked hard at school and won a place to study theology at King's College London. He loved fashion, so he worked part-time as a sales assistant for the legendary British designer Vivienne Westwood.

Creative genius

William's creative ideas changed Kylie's image and helped to re-launch her career. He was promoted from stylist to creative director. As well as styling Kylie's music videos and public appearances, he has directed award-winning shows such as *KylieFever2002*. Kylie's concerts have become famous for their breathtaking stage costumes, choreography and sets. In 2008, William won a style award from top fashion magazine *Elle*.

Meeting Kylie

In 1994, pop star Kylie Minogue came into the Vivienne Westwood boutique, and William asked her out for a coffee. Although William did not have any formal fashion training, he wowed Kylie with his style ideas. Over the next year, they became friends. His first official styling job came in 1995, when Kylie was due to perform with Nick Cave and the Bad Seeds on a primetime TV music show called *Top of the Pops*. William teamed Kylie's messy red hair with a green silk dress covered in beetles. Kylie invited William to style her for more performances and music videos, and her new looks made headlines over and over again.

In demand

Today, everyone wants to work with William. He has styled tours for other pop stars, including Britney Spears' *Circus* tour in 2009, and Leona Lewis' *Labyrinth* tour in 2010. William describes his job as 'a bit of everything. Photography, styling, directing shows and videos, writing… If I had to do just one of those things, I'd get frustrated.' His next project is a glittering musical featuring Kylie's greatest hits.

IMAGE MAKERS

A celebrity stylist works as a vital member of a large team to put together a fashion shoot. Once the look and approach of a shoot have been agreed, the stylist sources clothes, shoes and accessories.

When working on a celebrity shoot for a magazine, a stylist works closely with a team of editors, designers and stylists from the magazine to plan the perfect look.

The superstar

Celebrities know that fresh, eye-catching photographs will help interest fans in their latest work. The stylist provides a rack of clothes so that the celebrity can pick outfits that keep with the mood of the photoshoot.

The stylist

It's not just the celebrity that has to look good. A key part of a stylist's job is to make clothes and accessories look so desirable in the finished picture that people will want to buy them. They steam clothes to remove any creases, polish jewellery, and then help the celebrity to dress, pinning or sewing garments around the body for the very best fit.

The photographer

On the day of the shoot, the stylist works with the photographer to bring his or her vision to life. This includes styling the background and props, such as furniture or plants, to create the right mood and character.

The hair and make-up stylists

Hair and make-up complete the look that the celebrity stylist creates. The hair and make-up stylists take inspiration from the clothes, and must balance the latest trends with a style that suits the celebrity's complexion and face shape.

The fashion PR

Fashion PRs promote fashion brands. They lend clothes and accessories to stylists for free, in return for coverage in magazines. This is why celebrities are often photographed wearing the latest gear not yet in the shops.

STYLE PRO TIPS

Top stylists use accessories such as bags, belts and jewellery to maximum effect. They work with their clients to create looks that show off their best features. Celebrity stylists spend hours working with their clients to find a style that works for them. Try out these top tips to transform your own wardrobe.

1. Customise!

Great stylists carry a sewing kit so that they can customise an outfit by adding their own special touches. They may change buttons to immediately update a piece of clothing, or dramatically transform it by altering the neck- or hemline.

2. Vintage vibe

Celebrity stylists are often seen in vintage clothing shops, searching for hidden classic gems. They mix older items with the very latest accessories to create a fabulous vintage look that reflects the latest fashion trends.

3. Mix and match

Many stylists love mixing various shades and textures of the same colour. For instance, they may pair a navy suit with a slate-blue shirt and a blue tweed tie. The chosen shades and textures are subtly different so that they work together, but do not look as though the celebrity is wearing matching clothes from head to toe.

4. Shave and save

Fluff and loose thread can make a vintage piece of clothing look shabby. Stylists use a razor to shave the surface of old fabric. This gets rid of any loose threads or fluffy wool and breathes new life into a vintage gem.

5. Showing off!

Stylists focus on their clients' most attractive features. They'll emphasise a small waist by accentuating it with an eye-catching, colourful belt. If a celebrity has great legs, they'll show them off in a dazzling short skirt. While they follow trends, top stylists don't follow them to the letter – they shape their celebrities' outfits to work with trends in a way that flatters the client.

WORD ON STYLE

Add some style to your fashion speak with the Radar guide!

best-dressed lists

the lists compiled by magazines, newspapers and websites, picturing the most stylish celebrities at an event, or out and about. Being on these lists gives the celebrities good publicity

boutique

a small or speciality fashion store selling selected clothes and accessories

costume design

researching, designing and creating costumes for a character in TV shows, on film or on stage

creative director

someone who oversees every part of a performer's image, from clothes to the theme of his or her music and shows

custom made

something that has been made specifically for a celebrity

fashion director

the top stylist working on a magazine. The fashion director controls which clothes, models and brands make it into the magazine, and decides how they are presented to make them appealing to readers

fashion editor

a stylist working on a magazine or newspaper

fashion-forward

people, clothes or looks that are very fashionable and ahead of the trends

fashion PR

short for fashion public relations: the fashion PR is responsible for making sure that the fashion house is always presented in the best possible way and is usually the link between the fashion house and stylists

fashionista

someone who follows fashion very closely

fashion PR

short for fashion public relations: the fashion PR is responsible for making sure that the fashion house is always presented in the best possible way and is usually the link between the fashion house and stylists

Designer clothes are often sold in exclusive shops or boutiques.

personal stylist
a stylist who is paid to style people for public or private events, or everyday life, rather than for a photoshoot, film or TV show

props
portable things such as furniture or accessories that are used at a photoshoot

signature look
a trademark way of dressing for which a celebrity is known

tear sheets
examples of previous work in a stylist's portfolio

test shoot
a photoshoot that a stylist works on for free, to gain experience. The test shoot is not for publication, but helps the stylist to build a portfolio that will win him or her work in the future

vintage
original clothes or accessories from the past

GLOSSARY

Fashion editors can push the boundaries to make clothes as eye-catching as possible.

A-list
a real or imaginary list of the most 'important' individuals, especially in show business

aristocrats
members of the highest class in some societies

choreography
planning a sequence of dance moves

client
someone who pays a stylist to work for him or her

collaborating
working together to produce or create something

complexion
the natural colour, texture and appearance of a person's skin

corsets
close-fitting undergarments that support and shape the waistline, hips, and breasts

high-street fashion
clothing and accessories that are not exclusive to designer shops but can be bought in most cities

internship
a job (often unpaid), that helps someone to gain experience in an industry

paparazzi
the photographers who follow celebrities to get unofficial, unposed photographs of them

petticoats
thin slips or underskirts worn beneath skirts and dresses

source
to look for something

theology
the study of religion and religious beliefs

KATIE GRAND

Fashion's ultimate fan

THE STATS

Name: Katie Grand
Place of birth: Leeds, UK
Lives: London, UK
Job: Stylist, magazine editor and fashion consultant

Self-styled talent

Katie's passion for fashion started when she was 12. Her father bought her copies of the style magazines *Vogue* and *The Face*. Overnight, she changed from 'nerdy' child into a wannabe fashion designer. Katie was not good at art, but she took drawing and pottery classes to improve her design skills.

Getting into magazines

When Katie was 17, she wrote to the editor of *Vogue* to ask how to get a job. Katie followed the editor's advice and went to study at Central Saint Martin's College of Art and Design in London, UK. Before finishing her course, Katie left to work on the magazine *Dazed & Confused*. She worked there for seven years and so impressed the editors of rival magazine *The Face* that they gave her the job of fashion director.

High fashion

Katie hit the big time in 1998 when the luxury handbag company, Bottega Veneta, hired her to give them a new image. Katie used young designer Giles Deacon to turn their fashion shows into must-see events. Her work captured the attention of Prada, who hired Katie as their chief stylist. Katie went on to style adverts and catwalk shows for dozens of top designers. She has also put together cover-star looks for A-list celebrities such as Madonna, Kate Moss, Scarlett Johansson, Christina Ricci and Victoria Beckham.

Super stylist

Today, Katie is one of the most powerful stylists in the world, earning £3,000-£4,000 a day. She also runs her own style magazine, *LOVE*, for people who love fashion and design. Katie was offered a job designing handbags for Mulberry but she decided to stick with what she does best – being a stylist.

Career highlights

1984 read her first copy of *The Face*

1992 went to work on *Dazed & Confused* magazine

1999 became fashion director of *The Face*

2000 made Editor-in-Chief of fashion and art magazine *Pop*,

2005 named as one of the world's most powerful stylists by *The Daily Telegraph*

2009 launched the *LOVE* fashion magazine

Katie works in partnership with celebrities and designers and is one of the most powerful people in the fashion industry.

Explore Katie's stylish world at www.katiegrand.com

STYLE STORY

From kings and queens to the first movie stars, the rich and famous have always employed experts to help them dress well. During the twentieth century, stylists helped to sell clothes to the masses by making them look good on the catwalk and in magazines. Today, top stylists are some of the most influential people in fashion.

Charles Frederick Worth (1826–1895) was the first designer to advise and dress his aristocratic clients, including Elisabeth von Österreich, Empress of Austria (above).

Rich and famous

The first 'style consultants' were personal assistants who helped wealthy people to dress well. The best-dressed aristocrats set style trends that were copied by other wealthy people. Rich women wore custom-made outfits with many layers. They needed help to get dressed, from putting on enormous petticoats to fastening corsets. In the 1800s and early-1900s, photographs of society events appeared in early fashion magazines, showing the latest clothes worn by royalty and aristocrats. Before the age of professional models, readers looked at these celebrities to find out what was fashionable.

Shop the style

The invention of the sewing machine in the mid-1800s led to clothes that were sold 'ready-to-wear'. Department stores began to offer the services of personal shoppers, to help customers find clothes that suited them. They also used style consultants to help them order the most fashionable stock. In the 1910s, newspaper reporters invented the word 'stylist' to describe the job of Tobé Davis, a style expert who advised hundreds of department stores on what would be in fashion each season.

Fashion and film

From the 1930s, the most famous faces and figures in the world belonged to Hollywood movie stars and it soon became important for these celebrities to look good all the time. Since then, stylists have been in demand in Los Angeles, USA, but the 'celebrity stylist' phenomenon really exploded in the 1990s. Designers wanted the most famous actors to wear their clothes. The actors knew that a fashionable image would help them to get work. Stylists became the bridge between celebrity and designer, setting up deals between stars and fashion brands.

Power players

Today, top celebrity stylists such as Rachel Zoe (see below) are household names. Their celebrity partnerships give them huge power and influence in the fashion industry. In 2011, Lady Gaga's stylist Nicola Formichetti became the first stylist to be put in charge of design at a large fashion brand, when he was named the creative director of Thierry Mugler (a French fashion label).

Rachel Zoe is one of the most influential people in Hollywood fashion and employs a team of seven people to help get her celebrity looks just right.

The Rachel Zoe effect

Rachel Zoe tops the list of the world's most influential stylists. As well as dressing A-list clients such as Cameron Diaz and Anne Hathaway, Zoe consults for fashion brands, has written a best-selling book and stars in a reality TV show, *The Rachel Zoe Project*. She has even started her own fashion label, bringing her famous 'hippy-meets-vintage' style to the mass-market.

ALL GLAMOUR AND GLITZ?

Celebrity styling sounds like every fashion-lover's dream job. From the outside, it looks just as glamorous as being a celebrity. The benefits include:

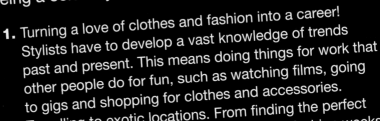

YES

1. Turning a love of clothes and fashion into a career! Stylists have to develop a vast knowledge of trends past and present. This means doing things for work that other people do for fun, such as watching films, going to gigs and shopping for clothes and accessories.
2. Travelling to exotic locations. From finding the perfect location for a photoshoot to jetting out to fashion weeks around the world, international travel is a must.
3. Being creative. Anyone can buy clothes, but celebrity stylists combine them in original and fashion-forward ways. Top stylists such as Katie Grand are so creative that their ideas influence designers.
4. Seeing your ideas and work in print. Successful stylists have the satisfaction of seeing the images they help to create in magazines, newspapers and fashion blogs.
5. Working with like-minded people. Stylists need contacts inside the fashion industry, including models, make-up artists, hair stylists, photographers and fashion PRs. Networking at fashion parties and events is a glamorous but also important part of the role.

NO

However, stylists are keen to point out how hard they work. It can be a long time before the job becomes glamorous. They argue that:

1. Many stylists start with unpaid work placements, such as magazine internships. They work with photographers on a large number of test shoots to get tear sheets and build a portfolio. It can be two years or more before you start making money.

2. Working in the world of photoshoots, films or TV shows can mean long days, tight deadlines and often working away from home on shoots. It is the stylist's job to fit in with the client's schedule. They can be on call for a demanding celebrity, or working 18 hours a day to prepare for a big event. All this leaves stylists little time for a social life of their own!

3. Celebrity stylists are responsible for everything that goes into a flawless look, including steaming clothes and keeping up with paperwork. Packing and lugging suitcases around is hard work. Stylists also need to learn how to sew, so they can make every item fit and look good on the body.

4. Not all style is about glamour. Indie bands such as Athlete and Starsailor hire stylists to create an 'unstyled' image! You won't find these stylists interviewed in the press or posing next to their clients on the red carpet.

YES OR NO?

Celebrity stylists work in a glamorous industry, but getting there takes effort, teamwork and years of experience. They are the ones mending clothes and doing the laundry, while their celebrity clients step out in the spotlight. But every top stylist loves their job because it gives them a chance to live and breathe style – and even shape fashion history themselves!

STYLE UP!

Fashion loves the next big thing, so why not put your style on the map? Follow Radar's fashion trail to get the buzz on careers in fashion styling.

Websites

The London College of Fashion
Visit the college that trained everyone, from shoe designer Jimmy Choo to fashion journalist Karen Kay. You can also book a ticket to go to their open days: **www.fashion.arts.ac.uk**

University of the Arts London Central Saint Martins
Follow in the footsteps of some of the world's leading stylists, including British *Vogue* editor Alexandra Shulman, at the most creative art school around: **www.csm.arts.ac.uk**

Fashion blogger Tavi Gevinson proves that it is never too early to get a foot on the fashion ladder. She started writing about fashion when she was 11, and was sitting on fashion show front-rows at 13: **www.thestylerookie.com**

Reads & Apps

Secrets of Stylists: An Insider's Guide to Styling the Stars by Sasha Charnin Morrison (Chronicle Books, 2011)

Style A to Zoe: The Art of Fashion, Beauty, & Everything Glamour by Rachel Zoe (Grand Central Publishing, 2007).

Style your own wardrobe using the *Stylebook*, *Touch Closet* and *StyleMixer* apps. All available from: **www.itunes.com https://market.android.com**

INDEX